# DK Watch me grow

# Duckling

DK

LONDON, NEW YORK, MUNICH,
MELBOURNE, and DELHI

Written and edited by Lisa Magloff
Designed by Sonia Whillock,
Mary Sandberg, and Sadie Thomas
Publishing Manager  Sue Leonard
Managing Art Editor  Clare Shedden
Jacket Design  Hedi Gutt
Jacket Design  Mariza O'Keeffe
Picture Researcher  Julia Harris Voss
Production  Lucy Baker
DTP Designer  Almudena Díaz
Consultant  Barbara Taylor

First American edition, 2003
First paperback edition, 2006
Published in the United States by
DK Publishing, Inc.
375 Hudson Street
New York, New York 10014

06 07 08 09 10 9 8 7 6 5 4 3

A Cataloging-in-Publication record for this book
is available from the Library of Congress

ISBN-13 978-0-7894-9628-7 (hardcover)
ISBN-10 0-7894-9628-3 (hardcover)
ISBN-13 978-0-7566-2212-1 (pbk.)
ISBN-10 0-7566-2212-3 (pbk.)

Come fly with us and watch us GROW!

Colour reproduction by GRB Editrice S.r.l., Verona, Italy.
Printed and bound by South China Printing Co, Ltd., China

Discover more at
**www.dk.com**

# Contents

# I'm a duck

I'm a great swimmer and I can fly, too! My body is covered with soft, oily feathers. I am completely waterproof.

**Look closely**
Can you see the water droplets rolling off the duck's oily feathers?

Ducks have soft feathers to keep them warm.

Ducks have a stretchy web of skin in between each long toe.

Ridges on a duck's bill help it grip its food.

Turn the page and find out how my life began.

Bottoms up Some ducks dip underwater to search for food. This is called dabbling.

Gobble......
Gurgle......
Slurp......

# Before I was born

Mom and Dad met in the spring and built a nest. Soon Mom laid her eggs, and I was in one of them.

**Together**
Male and female ducks stay together until their eggs are laid.

**Bright and beautiful**
Male ducks are very colorful. They attract female ducks by ruffling their own feathers.

This is my dad.

## Under cover

Female ducks are the same color as the nest. This helps them hide their eggs.

This is my mom.

## Nest-making

Duck parents use feathers, twigs, and grasses to build a cozy, warm nest.

# Inside my egg I'm warm and snug

My mom sits on our eggs to keep them warm. She sits on them night and day until it's time for us to hatch.

**Feather blanket**
The nest is lined with feathers to make it warm and soft. Inside the nest, the eggs are safe and snug.

# Watch out— danger about!

Duck eggs are a tasty treat for many animals, such as rats and foxes. The mother duck keeps a sharp lookout for hungry animals. When she spots one, she protects her eggs by chasing it away.

**Rat**

**Fox**

Tap... Tap... Crack... Crack...

Look at this egg. Can you see a tiny, pink beak?

Tap, tap, peek -a-boo toes.

Tap, tap, wait for me!

# It's time for me to break out

Inside the shell, I start to peck. It takes me about 10 hours to peck my way out of my shell.

Puff, pant, I'm nearly there.

Phew! Did it!

# I'm two days old

It's time to go for my first waddle. It's hard work. I make sure I stay close to Mom, so that she can look after me.

My brothers, sisters, and I have to run to keep up with Mom

Mother ducks watch for any signs of danger.

She likes to take such big, strong steps!

## walkabout facts

🦆 Ducks have no nerves in their feet, so their toes never get cold, even on icy ponds.

🦆 Ducks' feet are made of the same bendy stuff that is in your nose and ears.

# I'm off for my first swim

After three days, I make my way
to the water, where I start to paddle.
My feathers are waterproof, and they
keep me warm and dry.

## Did you know?

When baby ducklings get cold,
they huddle close to their mom
to warm up.

## Paddle power
Duckling's flat feet push them along in the water.

*Paddle hard, my little ones!*

## Two weeks old
The duckling's beak is growing longer and it has lost all of its fluffy yellow feathers.

15

# I'm four weeks old

It's fun to catch my own meals
by dipping under the water.
My flat beak helps me scoop
up lots of food.

A duckling
cannot fly
because its
wings are
not fully
grown yet.

### Yummy dinner
Guess what? This
is a duck's dinner!
Millions of tiny insects
and tasty green
plants are floating
around in the pond.

\_\_\_\_\_Webbed feet help ducks balance in the water.

## Gobble facts

. . . . . . . . . . . . . . . . . . . . . . . . . .

🦆 Ducks are mostly vegetarian. They eat mainly plants and seeds that grow in or near the water.

🦆 Foods like bread and cookies are bad for ducks because they swell up in their stomachs. Ouch!

# I'm ready to fly

I'm eight weeks old and my wings are fully grown. I can't wait to fly with the other ducks. But first I have to learn how to take off and land.

When they take off, ducks tilt their wings and flap very fast.

A duck's tail feathers help it steer.

Up, up, and away—I feel as light as a feather!

A final push and the duck lifts into the air.

## Flying together

When they travel long distances, ducks always fly with other ducks. A group of ducks is called a flock.

# The circle of life goes around and around

Now you know how I turned into a fluffy duck.

# My friends from around the world

This is a White-Faced Duck from South Africa.

American Wood Ducks like to build their nests in trees close to water.

Pekin Ducks have fluffy yellow chicks.

The Black-Bellied Whistling Duck makes a sound like "pe-che-che."

There are hundreds of different kinds of ducks in the world. Are there any ducks living near you?

Mandarin Ducks live in China and like to eat rice and other grains.

The Shoveler Duck uses its big bill to dig for food.

**phwee-eek**

The Plumed Whistler makes a sound just like a squeaky whistle.

## FuN duck facts

. . . . . . . . . . . . . . . . . . . . . . . . .

🦆 The Black Brant Duck can fly more than 960 miles (1,600 kilometers) without stopping.

🦆 Most ducks fly south in the fall, so they can spend the winter in a warm place.

🦆 Male ducks are usually more colorful than female ducks.

# Glossary

### Feathers
Soft, light parts that cover the outside of a bird's body.

### Hatching
When a baby duck or other animal comes out of its egg.

### Waterproof
Something that does not let water pass through it.

### Nest
A place that a duck builds out of twigs to lay its eggs in.

### Webbing
The thin skin between a duck's toes.

### Dabbling
When ducks feed by sticking their heads under water.

## Acknowledgments
The publisher would like to thank the following for their kind permission to reproduce their photographs:
(Key: a=above; c=centre; b=below; l=left; r=right; t=top)
1: Windrush Photos/Colin Carver c; 2: Masterfile UK c; 2-3: N.H.P.A./Manfred Danegger b; 3: Ardea London Ltd/Tom & Pat Leeson tr; 4: Ardea London Ltd/John Daniels bl; Pat Morris tr; 4-5: Global PhotoSite Copyright © 2000 - 2003 Chris Edwards/Mal Smith cl; 5: Global PhotoSite Copyright © 2000 - 2003 Chris Edwards/Mal Smith tr; 5: Oxford Scientific Films br; 6: Ardea London Ltd/Kenneth W. Fink tr; 6-7: Holt Studios/Primrose Peacock; 7: Oxford Scientific Films/ Mark Hamblin br; 8: Premaphotos Wildlife/KG Preston-Mafham l; 8-9: FLPA - Images of Nature/Maurice Walker; 10-11: Premaphotos Wildlife/K G Preston-Mafham c; 12-13: Oxford Scientific Films/ Wendy Shattil and Bob Rozinski; 14-15: Ardea London Ltd/Brian Bevan, 15: Ardea London Ltd/John Daniels tr; 15: FLPA - Images of nature/Tony Wharton br; 16: Ardea London Ltd/John Daniels l; 17: Ardea London Ltd/John Daniels; 18: Ardea London Ltd/John Daniels; 19: Ardea London Ltd/Chris Knights c; John Daniels bl; 20: Ardea London Ltd/John Daniels tl, br, bra; 20: Chris Gomersall Photography cl; 20: Holt Studios/Wayne Hutchinson c; 21: FLPA - Images of nature/Jurgen & Christine Sohns; 22: Ardea London Ltd/Jim Zipp 2000 bl; Kenneth W. Fink cla; 22: Holt Studios/Mike Lane tr; 23: Ardea London Ltd/ Kenneth W. Fink tr; 23: Getty Images/Richard Coomber tl; 23: Masterfile UK br; 24: Ardea London Ltd/John Daniels bl; Pat Morris cl; 24: Windrush Photos/David Tipling br. Jacket Front: Barrie Watts tcr, Ardea/John Daniels bc.
All other images © Dorling Kindersley
For further information see: www.dkimages.com